Plastic Timeline

1856

Alexander Parkes uses cellulose from plants to invent Parkesine.

1897

Casein plastic, made from milk, is invented in Germany.

1880

Plastic replaces animal horn and tortoiseshell as the most popular material for making combs.

1870

John Wesley Hyatt patents a plastic called celluloid.

1907

Bakelite is invented by Leo Baekeland. It is the first synthetic plastic.

1892

A semisynthetic fiber called rayon is made from cellulose.

1956

The first cooking pans with a nonstick plastic coating are manufactured.

1935

A plastic fiber called nylon is invented by Wallace Carothers.

2011

The new Boeing 787 airliner has more plastic parts than any other airliner before.

1932

Perspex, also known as plexiglass, is invented. It is used as a replacement for glass.

2001

Helios, an experimental unmanned airplane made mainly of plastic, reaches world record height of 96,863 feet (29,524 meters).

1940

A new synthetic rubber helps supply huge numbers of rubber tires during World War II.

What Is Plastic?

UNIT

Hydrogen atom

Carbon atom

POLYMER

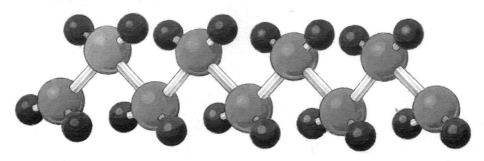

Plastic is a material such as nylon, PVC, or polythene that can be molded into a new shape while it is soft. It then sets, keeping its new shape. The word *plastic* comes from the Greek word *plastikos*, meaning "able to be molded or shaped."

Everything you can see and touch is made of invisibly tiny particles called atoms. They're so small that you can't see them, no matter how good your eyesight is. Atoms often join together in small groups called molecules. Most molecules contain just a few atoms. Plastic is different. It's made of very long molecules. Each molecule looks like a length of bicycle chain. It has hundreds or thousands of identical units joined together to form a long chain called a polymer. These long chains can slide over each other, making the plastic soft and easily shaped when it is hot, and then they link together when it cools, locking in the new plastic shape.

Author:

Ian Graham earned a degree in applied physics at City University, London. He then took a graduate diploma in journalism. Since becoming a freelance author and journalist, he has written more than 250 children's nonfiction books.

Artist:

David Antram was born in Brighton, England, in 1958. He studied at Eastbourne College of Art and then worked in advertising for 15 years before becoming a full-time artist. He has illustrated many children's nonfiction books.

Series creator:

David Salariya was born in Dundee, Scotland. He has illustrated a wide range of books and has created and designed many new series for publishers in the UK and overseas. David established The Salariya Book Company in 1989. He lives in Brighton, England, with his wife, illustrator Shirley Willis, and their son, Jonathan.

Editor: **Caroline Coleman**

Editorial Assistant: **Mark Williams**

Published in Great Britain in 2016 by
The Salariya Book Company Ltd
25 Marlborough Place, Brighton BN1 1UB

ISBN-13: 978-0-531-21929-4 (lib. bdg.) 978-0-531-22053-5 (pbk.)

All rights reserved.
Published in 2016 in the United States
by Franklin Watts
An imprint of Scholastic Inc.
Published simultaneously in Canada.

A CIP catalog record for this book is available
from the Library of Congress.

Printed and bound in China.
Printed on paper from sustainable sources.
1 2 3 4 5 6 7 8 9 10 R 25 24 23 22 21 20 19 18 17 16

SCHOLASTIC, FRANKLIN WATTS, and associated logos are trademarks and/or registered trademarks of Scholastic Inc.

PAPER FROM
SUSTAINABLE
FORESTS

You Wouldn't Want to Live Without™
Plastic!

Written by
Ian Graham

Illustrated by
David Antram

Series created by
David Salariya

Franklin Watts®
An Imprint of Scholastic Inc.

Contents

Introduction 5

A World Without Plastic? 6

Before Plastic 8

The First Plastics 10

Science to the Rescue! 12

Plastics Take Off 14

Into the Space Age 16

It's a Plastic World! 18

Plastic Fantastic! 20

Make It From Plastic 22

Super Strength 24

Plastic Problems 26

Looking Into the Future 28

Glossary 30

Index 32

Introduction

Look around your home or school and you'll see plastic everywhere. It's in your computer, cell phone, television set, toys, games, pens, sports equipment, and even the books you read. Your clothes, carpets, furniture, and even the paint on your walls probably contain plastic, too. Look in your kitchen. You'll find a lot of plastic there. Plastic plays such an important part in everyone's life today that it's difficult to imagine what the world would be like without it. Many of the things you do every day would be different, or more difficult, or maybe even impossible if plastic had never been invented. And many of the things you buy would be much more expensive without it. You really wouldn't want to live without plastic.

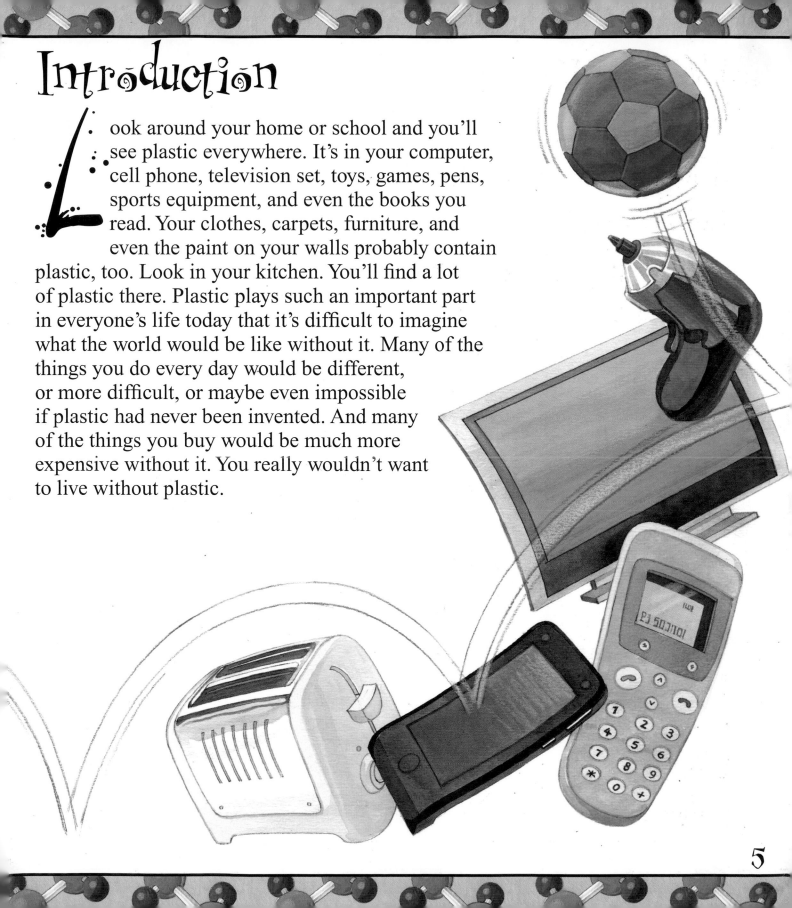

A World Without Plastic?

Today, so many of the things we use either are made of plastic or have some plastic parts. There are lots of different types of plastic. Some are soft, others are hard. Some are see-through, others aren't. Some are smooth and glossy, others are dull and rough. And plastic items can be made in white, black, and every color of the rainbow. The story was very different just over a hundred years ago. The many different types of plastic we have today hadn't been invented yet. Can you imagine what it would be like if plastic had never been invented? We might not have things like cell phones, computers, or the Internet.

HOPE YOU LIKE BAGGY CLOTHES! Without plastic, the synthetic fibers that give modern clothes their stretchiness would not exist.

BEFORE PLASTIC, glue was often made by boiling up animal hooves and hides. Most modern glues contain some form of plastic.

WITHOUT PLASTIC, you probably wouldn't have computers, cell phones, or game consoles, because so many of their parts are made of plastic.

PLASTIC FURNITURE can be made in almost any shape. Some shapes would be difficult to make as easily or cheaply from other materials. Some couldn't be made at all.

A home without plastic

Horse hooves were used to make glue because they contain keratin (as do your fingernails!). When hooves are melted in boiling water and acid is added, the keratin melts and forms thick, jelly-like glue.

Wool

Cotton

Brass

Paper

Cotton

Cotton

Glass

Wood

Leather

Wood

Wool

Wood

Before Plastic

Plastic was not common in people's homes until the 1950s. Before then, nearly everything is made of traditional materials such as wood, metal, stone, glass, leather, and natural fibers. Small items like buttons and knife handles are made from ivory, horn, and antler. These materials have been used for thousands of years. They have to be collected from wherever they can be found in nature and then processed to change them into useful things. The people who process them have years of experience in working with natural materials. They know about each material's strengths and weaknesses. However, plastic is about to change all of this.

Wood for building

Wool for making clothes

PIANO KEYS used to be made of ivory from elephant tusks. Playing a piano was known as "tickling the ivories." Ivory from one tusk could make 45 keyboards.

BEFORE COMBS were made of plastic, they were made of bone or antler. Their teeth were brittle and often snapped off. Plastic combs have flexible teeth that last longer.

Antler for making tools

Bone for making tools

Animal skin for making clothes

You Can Do It!

Clothes have care labels that tell you which fabrics the clothes are made of and how they should be cleaned. Can you find these labels in your clothes?

SHRINKING can be a problem when washing clothes made of natural fibers, especially woolen items. Clothes with synthetic fibers can endure repeated washing.

SITTING PRETTY.
Cushions, chairs, and soft toys used to be stuffed with straw, wool, wood shavings, sawdust, feathers, and horsehair. Today plastic fibers and foam are used.

The First Plastics

The first plastics are made from natural materials. One of the strangest is shellac. It is made from a substance called lac, which is produced by an insect, the lac bug. About 100,000 lac bugs produce 1 pound (500 grams) of shellac. Shellac can be molded to form all kinds of different shapes. The first sound recordings in the early 1900s are on records made of shellac. Another early plastic is Parkesine, patented in 1856 by Alexander Parkes. Parkesine is made from cellulose, a substance that comes from plants. The first photographic film is made from long strips of a clear plastic called celluloid, patented in 1870. One plastic is even made from milk! If modern plastics had not been created, we might still be using plastics made from natural materials.

SHELLAC RECORDS are very popular, but very brittle. Many of them end up cracked and broken. Plastic vinyl discs introduced in the 1930s are not so brittle, so they last much longer. They quickly replace shellac discs.

THE LAC BUG produces a red liquid called lac, which hardens on tree branches to form a glassy red material. It is collected, purified, and processed to make shellac.

Thank you!

It's shellac, from little bugs!

You Can Do It!

Ask an adult to heat a cup of milk.* Don't let it boil. Add two tablespoons of clear vinegar. Stir until lumps appear. When cool, squish them together. You've made milk plastic!

SAFETY: Be very careful not to splash or spill hot milk!

THE FIRST PHOTOGRAPHS are made one by one, on metal plates or sheets of glass. Celluloid film makes it possible to take photographs quickly enough to produce the first movies.

BRITISH QUEEN MARY (1867–1953) owns plastic jewelry made from milk! Milk contains a substance called casein. This is processed to make plastic called casein plastic or Galalith.

11

Science to the Rescue!

In the early 1900s, scientists start looking for new ways to make plastics. Instead of processing natural materials, they combine chemicals to make new ones. These plastics, created by scientists in laboratories, are called synthetic plastics. The first synthetic plastic in 1907 is named Bakelite after its inventor, Leo Baekeland. By the 1920s, radios, cameras, jewelry, light switches, electrical plugs, and clocks are being made from Bakelite. In the 1930s, Wallace Carothers creates a famous plastic called nylon, which is still in use today.

SHIRTS MADE OF NYLON are popular, but not for long. Electric charges build up on the fibers and give you an electric shock when you touch something metal, like a door handle. Ouch!

New Uses for Plastic

BAKELITE ARRIVES just as an invention called radio becomes popular. Millions of Bakelite radios are sold from 1920 to 1950, before television becomes widely available.

SO MANY THINGS are made of Bakelite that it becomes known as "the material of a thousand uses." You can even have a coffin made of Bakelite!

SOME PLASTICS created in the early 1900s are still used today. Look inside any small machine and you'll probably find gearwheels and other parts made of nylon.

WALLACE CAROTHERS (1896–1937) was an American chemist credited with the invention of nylon.

Wallace Carothers

Nylon fibers

13

Plastics Take Off

During World War II (1939–1945), all sorts of materials are in short supply, including rubber. Scientists are given the job of creating a new material that can be used instead of natural rubber. They succeed in making a stretchy rubberlike plastic. They manufacture other new plastics, too, such as Kodel, Terylene, and Dacron. After the war, millions of people are rebuilding their lives in new homes. Factories start making all the products they need, using the new plastics created in the 1930s and 1940s. It is around this time that plastic bottles begin to replace glass bottles. Plastics really take off.

THERE ISN'T ENOUGH natural rubber to make tires and other rubber parts for all the trucks, planes, and machines used during World War II. Scientists create synthetic rubber to solve the problem.

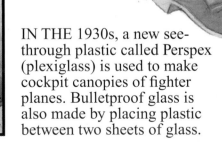

IN THE 1930s, a new see-through plastic called Perspex (plexiglass) is used to make cockpit canopies of fighter planes. Bulletproof glass is also made by placing plastic between two sheets of glass.

DANGER! Before bottles were made of plastic, they were made of thick, heavy glass. These bottles shatter if they are dropped or knocked over. Plastic bottles are much safer—they bounce!

You Can Do It!

Are any parts of your toys not made of plastic? Why do you think they aren't plastic? They might have to be stronger, harder, or springier than the plastic parts. Or is there another reason?

MORE DANGER! Playing with toys wouldn't be so safe if plastic had not been invented. Toys were once made of tinplate and lead. Tinplate has sharp edges and lead is poisonous.

Ouch!

Into the Space Age

Mass-produced plastic products reach shops in the 1950s just as the first spaceflights hit the headlines. Plastic is a space-age material for a space-age world. After the dark days of World War II, plastic makes everyone feel that the future has arrived. The first plastic products break more easily than sturdy wood and metal products, and they can't be repaired as easily, but it doesn't matter because new plastic products are less expensive. It's the beginning of our "throwaway" lifestyle. Instead of repairing something, we throw it away and buy something new to replace it.

A PLASTIC HOOP called a hula hoop is a must-have toy in the late 1950s. The idea is to spin it around your waist and keep it going by swiveling your hips.

THE FIRST TRANSISTOR RADIOS, made of plastic, appear in the 1950s. Their sound quality isn't great, but they are very popular among young people, because they are so small and portable.

Mix one tablespoon of cornstarch with one tablespoon of water. Stir in a tablespoon of white craft glue (this contains plastic polymer.) Let it set and it will turn into plastic slime.

BEFORE THE 1960s, dolls' heads were often made of china or porcelain. They broke very easily, so they had to be handled carefully. Plastic dolls are much tougher, so they last longer.

THE FIRST MODERN CREDIT CARDS are issued in the United States in the 1950s. These plastic cards make it easier for people to buy new products from stores.

17

It's a Plastic World!

There are thousands of different plastics for making all sorts of products. Think of all the gadgets you enjoy using. Your game console, laptop, tablet computer, and headphones all depend on plastic. Many of them have plastic cases, buttons, and switches. The electronic circuits inside them depend on plastic, too. The circuits are built on circuit boards made of plastic. Their microchips are sealed in plastic blocks. All kinds of electrical equipment, from table lamps to vacuum cleaners, work safely because of plastic. Their electrical wiring is covered with plastic to stop electric currents from escaping. Without plastic, life would be truly shocking. ZAP!

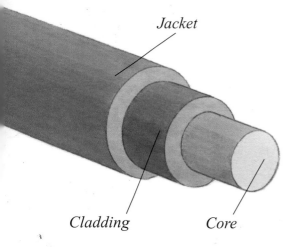

STICK WITH IT. Many of the glues used today, from craft glue to superglue, contain plastic polymers. As the glue sets, its long polymer chains lock together.

Jacket

Cladding   *Core*

LIGHT PIPES. The cables that carry telephone calls and computer information were once made of metal. Now, many of them are made of thin strands of glass or plastic called optical fibers.

THE GLOSSY PAPER used for printing photographs and magazine covers is coated with plastic to make it supersmooth and shiny. The coating is also designed to help colored ink stick to the paper.

PARACHUTES, yacht sails, and hot-air balloons are made of a very strong plastic fabric called ripstop. Its fibers are woven together to make a fabric that will not rip or tear easily.

ULTRALIGHTWEIGHT PLASTIC has made it possible to build aircraft that were impossible to make in the past. Helios was an electric plane powered by the energy in sunlight.

How It Works

Plastic circuit boards are covered with metal tracks. The tracks work like wires and connect the different parts of a circuit to each other.

Plastic Fantastic!

If it weren't for plastic, you'd have to work a lot harder at home. Smooth plastic surfaces are easy to clean with a wipe. Old wooden kitchen tables had to be scrubbed with disinfectant to keep them clean. Modern nonstick saucepans are easier to clean than old iron or enamel pans. In the bathroom, toothbrushes with plastic bristles are easier to clean than old brushes made of animal hair. Modern paints and varnishes contain plastic, giving them a durable, long-lasting, easy-to-clean surface. Without plastic, you'd have to repaint surfaces more often and spend much more time cleaning them. Plastic makes life much easier.

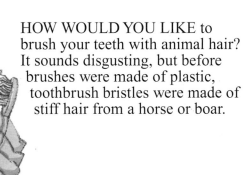

HOW WOULD YOU LIKE to brush your teeth with animal hair? It sounds disgusting, but before brushes were made of plastic, toothbrush bristles were made of stiff hair from a horse or boar.

IRON AND STEEL turn to rust if they get wet. They have to be polished or painted to protect them. Plastic doesn't rust, so it doesn't have to be polished or painted.

Iron and steel turn to rust because of a chemical reaction between the metal, water, and oxygen in the air. Plastic doesn't rust because it doesn't react chemically with water and oxygen.

Iron chain

Plastic chain

OUTDOORS in damp weather, wood can rot quickly unless protected with a coat of preservative, varnish, or paint. Now, there are doors and window frames made of plastic.

A STICKY PROBLEM. If there were no plastic sticky tape, you'd have to make do with tape made of paper or fabric. Paper tears and fabric tape is thick and ugly.

21

Make It From Plastic

About 280 million tons (250 million metric tons) of plastic is made every year. Newly made plastic looks like brightly colored gravel. To make things from it, it is heated until it melts. Chemicals may be added to make it harder, softer, or a different color. Gas may be blown into it to make foam plastic. The hot plastic is forced into a mold. The mold is cooled to harden the plastic. One molding machine can make hundreds or even thousands of identical plastic products a day. A variety of different manufacturing methods are used, including injection molding, extrusion, drawing, and blow molding.

DRAWING. Fibers are made by forcing hot plastic through tiny holes in a disc called a spinneret (right). Cold water hardens the fibers.

Plastic granules go in

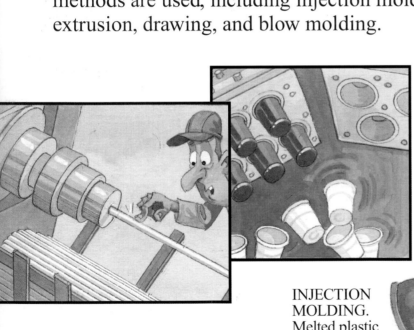

EXTRUSION. Melted plastic is forced through a die (metal block) with a large hole in it. Plastic rods, bars, and pipes are made like this.

INJECTION MOLDING. Melted plastic is forced into a mold. Cold water cools the mold. It splits open and the perfectly formed plastic product falls out into a waiting bin.

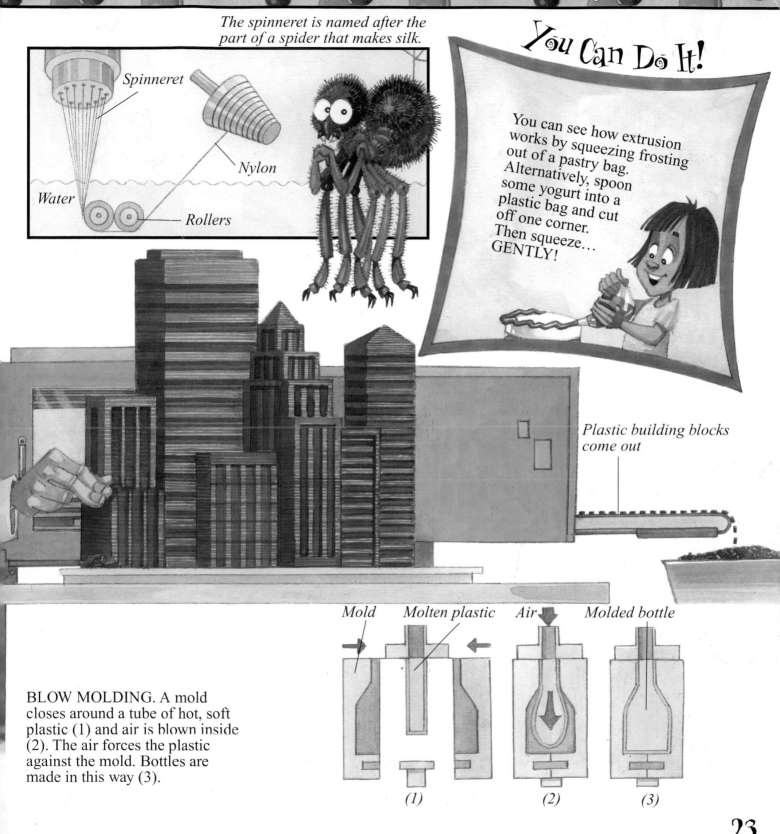

The spinneret is named after the part of a spider that makes silk.

Spinneret

Nylon

Water

Rollers

You can see how extrusion works by squeezing frosting out of a pastry bag. Alternatively, spoon some yogurt into a plastic bag and cut off one corner. Then squeeze... GENTLY!

Plastic building blocks come out

Mold   Molten plastic   Air   Molded bottle

BLOW MOLDING. A mold closes around a tube of hot, soft plastic (1) and air is blown inside (2). The air forces the plastic against the mold. Bottles are made in this way (3).

(1)   *(2)*   *(3)*

23

Carbon Fiber

1. MATS of woven carbon fiber are laid in a mold and soaked in resin (liquid plastic).

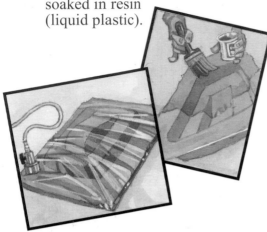

2. THE MOLD is sealed inside a plastic bag and the air is sucked out to squash the layers together.

3. THE MOLD, in the plastic bag, is heated in an oven called an autoclave to harden the plastic.

4. WHEN THE AUTOCLAVE has cooled down, the finished carbon fiber part can be taken out. The plastic resin has set, locking the carbon fiber mats together.

Super Strength

Some plastics are strong enough to stop a bullet. Some of them are fireproof, too. These plastics are used to make superstrong clothing to protect motorcyclists, firefighters, and auto-racing drivers. Ordinary plastics can be made stronger by combining them with another material. The new material is called a composite. Plastic composites are stronger than each of the materials they contain. Carbon fiber reinforced plastic, also known as carbon fiber, is a composite material ten times stronger and four times lighter than steel. Sports equipment such as tennis rackets, golf clubs, and ice hockey sticks are often made of carbon fiber. It's used to make race cars, too.

COMPOSITE MATERIALS are replacing metal parts in airliners. The Boeing 787 Dreamliner (below) has more composite parts than any other airliner. Half of its body and wings are made of composites.

*Superstrong
fireproof suit*

Carbon fiber is such a strong material because of all the fibers inside it. When something tries to bend it, the plastic spreads the force across lots of fibers.

*Carbon fiber
car body*

SMOOTH BOATS made of carbon fiber slip through the water easily and quickly. The worms, barnacles, and other sea life that often damage wooden boats can't get a grip on supersmooth plastic.

Plastic Problems

Plastic has great advantages, but it also has problems. In time, plastic parts and products break, wear out, or just become unfashionable and have to be replaced. Old unwanted wood, food, and natural fibers rot and eventually dissolve and disappear. Discarded plastic, however, can last for hundreds of years before it breaks down. One way to stop it piling up in landfills, and polluting the earth and water as it breaks down, is to use it again to make new things. This is called recycling. Another way is to burn it in a power station to make electricity.

OCEAN CURRENTS go around and around in circles in two parts of the Pacific Ocean, trapping garbage in the middle (right). A lot of it is plastic.

Hmmm. That looks tasty!

ANIMALS might prefer a world without plastic. Countless turtles and seabirds have been killed by eating plastic in the sea, because they don't know it's bad for them.

LARGE plastic containers are reused as water carriers in developing countries. The lightweight plastic enables people to carry water over long distances a little more easily.

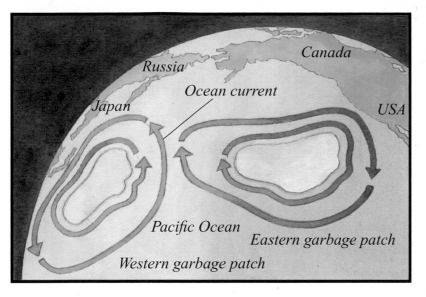

Russia
Canada
Ocean current
Japan
USA
Pacific Ocean
Eastern garbage patch
Western garbage patch

You Can Do It!

Look for triangular recycling marks on plastic bottles in your home. Make a note of the different plastics you find. Which is the most common?

DID YOU KNOW that you might be wearing recycled plastic? Plastic drink bottles are recycled to make the fibers that produce fleece jackets. It takes 25 plastic bottles to make one jacket.

PLASTIC BOTTLES can be recycled by being used to help build houses. The bottles are filled with sand or mud. Empty bottles can also be used to build greenhouses for growing plants.

DIFFERENT PLASTICS need to be recycled separately, so recyclers need to know which plastics they have. Some products have a triangle mark with a number to show the type of plastic. For example, 6 = PS = polystyrene. It's called the Resin Identification Code.

Resin Identification Codes

1	2	3	4	5	6	7
PETE	HDPE	V	LDPE	PP	PS	Other

27

Looking Into the Future

Scientists are still creating new plastics and improving old ones. Most plastics are made from chemicals that come from oil, but oil causes pollution, and it will run out one day. Don't worry, you won't have to do without plastic. Future plastics will probably be made from natural materials, just as the first plastics were. They are called bioplastics. They're made from starch and cellulose produced by plants. Some bottles, packaging, and car parts already contain bioplastics. There are also new plastics that "heal" when they are cut. Products made from them will never show scratches. You'll wonder how we ever lived without plastic!

New Technologies

CLEVER PACKAGING. There are new plastics that change color when bacteria grow on them. Food packaging made of this plastic will tell you if the food inside is no longer safe to eat.

PRINT IT. Already people can make small plastic objects by using a 3D printer to print them. The printer makes things by building up one layer of plastic on top of another.

BENDY SCREENS. Nearly all screens on computers and other devices are made of hard, flat glass or plastic. Future plastic screens might be as thin and flexible as a sheet of paper.

Top Tip

Recycling plastic saves energy. It takes only about a quarter of the energy to make a plastic bottle from recycled plastic as it does to make the same bottle from new materials.

It's for making plastic!

PLASTIC MONEY. Australia, Canada, and New Zealand have changed from paper banknotes to plastic. More countries are likely to join them. Plastic banknotes last longer than paper.

Glossary

3D Three-dimensional: having length, width, and depth.

Atom The smallest particle of a chemical element.

Bacteria Microscopic living organisms. Many kinds of bacteria are harmless or useful to us, but some are dangerous because they cause diseases.

Blow molding A way of forming hollow plastic objects like bottles by closing a mold around a tube of hot, soft plastic, and blowing air inside.

Canopy A covering such as the see-through top of a fighter plane's cockpit.

Casein A substance found in milk.

Cellulose A substance found in plant fibers and the walls of plant cells.

Composite material A material made by combining two or more materials, such as carbon fiber reinforced plastic.

Disinfectant A cleaning product, usually liquid, that kills bacteria.

Drawing A way of forming fibers by forcing plastic, or another substance, through tiny holes in a block of metal.

Electronic circuit A pathway along which an electric current can flow, usually through a series of electronic devices that use the electrical energy to do work.

Extrusion A way of forming plastic rods, bars, and pipes by forcing hot, soft plastic through a block of metal with a large hole in it.

Factory A building or buildings where products are manufactured.

Fiber A thread of natural material (such as cotton) or synthetic material (such as nylon or rayon).

Gearwheel A toothed wheel. Also known as a gear or cog, usually found in small machines.

Injection molding A way of forming plastic by forcing hot liquid plastic into a mold and then cooling it.

Lifestyle A way of living for one person or a group of people.

Manufacture To make products for sale, usually in large numbers.

Microchip A small package of electronic parts forming one or more electronic circuits in one small block of plastic. Also called a chip, integrated circuit, or IC.

Molecule A group of atoms linked together.

Monomer A molecule that is linked to lots of other identical molecules to form a long, chain-like molecule called a polymer.

Oxygen One of the gases in air. Oxygen makes up about 20 percent (a fifth) of the air you breathe. Most of the rest is another gas called nitrogen.

Pollution Unwanted and sometimes harmful substances in the environment, especially in the air or water.

Polymer A long, chain-like molecule made of lots of identical units called monomers linked together.

Space age The period of history that began with the first spaceflight on October 4, 1957.

Starch A natural substance found in plants.

Superglue A very strong, quick-setting glue made of a plastic polymer called cyanoacrylate.

Synthetic Made artificially, by combining substances in a way that does not happen in nature.

Tinplate Thin sheets of iron or steel coated with a layer of tin.

Index

A
antler 8
autoclave 24

B
Baekeland, Leo 12
Bakelite 12
banknotes 29
bioplastics 28
blow molding 22, 23
boats 25
Boeing 787 Dreamliner 24
bone 8
bulletproof glass 14

C
carbon fiber 24
Carothers, Wallace 12
casein plastic 11
celluloid 10, 11
clothes 6, 9
comb 8
composite 24
cotton 7
credit cards 17

D
drawing 22

E
electrical equipment 18, 19
extrusion 22, 23

F
fibers
 natural 8, 9
 synthetic 6, 9, 12, 23, 24, 25
film 10, 11
foam plastic 22

G
Galalith 11
glue 6, 7, 18

H
Helios plane 19
horn 8
hula hoop 16

I
injection molding 22
iron 20, 21
ivory 8

L
lead 15

M
making plastic 22, 23
molding 22, 24

N
nonstick saucepan 20
nylon 12, 13

O
optical fibers 18

P
parachute 18
Parkes, Alexander 10
Parkesine 10
Perspex 14
plastic bottles 14, 15, 23
plastic slime 17
plexiglass 14
pollution 26, 27

R
records (discs) 10
recycling 26, 27, 29
resin 24
resin identification codes 27
rubber 14
rust 20, 21

S
shellac 10, 11
spinneret 22, 23
steel 20, 21
sticky tape 21

T
3D printer 28
tinplate 15
toothbrush 20
traditional materials 8

W
wood 7, 16, 21, 26
wool 7, 9
World War II 14

Top Inventors of Plastic

Alexander Parkes (1813–1890)
Parkes was born in Birmingham, England. He worked at a metal casting company that made things by pouring molten metal into molds. He dreamed up dozens of inventions, including new ways to process metal and strengthen it. Then, in 1841, he invented a way of using rubber to make fabric waterproof. Fifteen years later, he invented the plastic that was named after him, Parkesine.

Leo Baekeland (1863–1944)
Leo Henricus Arthur Backeland was born in Ghent, Belgium. He studied chemistry and became a chemistry professor. In 1891, he moved to the United States, and two years later he invented a new type of photographic paper. In 1897, he became an American citizen. Then he experimented with chemicals to make new materials. In 1909, he announced his invention of Bakelite and set up a company to make Bakelite products. He retired in 1939 and died five years later at the age of 80.

Wallace Carothers (1896–1937)
Wallace Hume Carothers was born in Burlington, Iowa. He excelled in chemistry in college and went to work for the DuPont chemical company. There, he led a team of scientists who invented a synthetic rubber called Neoprene in 1930. Five years later he invented nylon.

Fire!

The first movies were photographed on film made from a plastic called celluloid. One of celluloid's disadvantages is that it catches fire very easily and burns quickly. When it burns, it produces poisonous smoke. Even if celluloid doesn't catch fire, it breaks down chemically over time. The clear film turns yellow, becomes sticky, and blisters. Eventually it falls apart altogether. The older it is, the more dangerous it becomes. It can even explode without warning! It's so dangerous that it can't even be thrown away. It has to be dealt with by experts. The oldest movies are kept in special fireproof storerooms until they can be copied onto modern film or recorded digitally.

A safer plastic film replaced celluloid in the 1940s. It was known as safety film. Although safety film doesn't burst into flames, it has another problem. After a few years, it begins to break down, giving off the telltale smell of vinegar. As the film breaks down it shrinks and becomes brittle. Colors on the film begin to fade, too. Films photographed on safety film can be rescued by copying them onto new film or recording them digitally.

Did You Know?

- On July 14, 2007, a floating bridge 118 feet (36 m) long was built from 14,100 empty 4-pint plastic milk bottles across the River Ouse in the city of Ely in England. It was the world's longest plastic-bottle bridge. The mayor of Ely then tested the bridge by walking across it.

- Every year, between 500 billion and 1 trillion plastic bags are used worldwide. That's more than a million a minute!

- Plastic takes so long to break down that nearly every piece of plastic ever made still exists today.

- DNA, the molecule inside our bodies' cells that carries the code that controls our growth and development, is a natural polymer. The longest DNA polymers are huge. They can be hundreds of billions of units long.

- A 3D printer can build a plastic model of almost any three-dimensional shape—even a model of yourself.